Contents

Delivered · Feb · 1st 2018 ·

"Pro Patria
Dimicans"
(Striving for One's Country)

From left to right: Roy (Me), Thomas (Dad),
Donald, Sydney, Eric, Elizabeth Rose (Mum)

Mere Memories

Take a trip back with me to a time just before World War 2. Memories spring jumbled into the present. They can be, none the less, interesting when set out in some reasonable order. Come, share a few of them now. These are mere tokens of school days spent at one of the Colleges founded by the redoubtable Canon Woodard. The particular school in question is no mere figment of the imagination, it thrives in the Shropshire countryside where a number of lakes, locally called "Meres," bring added beauty to rich farmland. Ellesmere, one of these tree lined lakes, and the biggest, gives its name to the town on its shore. It therefore names the College a mile or so beyond. This is the source of "Mere Memories."

The prelude to these flashbacks, before Ellesmere College makes its vast impact on me, is in another place around Christmas time, a little while before the Second Great War. You might well ask "Why at Christmas?" The answer, to be precise, begins in the preceding term but its effect hit home at that festive season.

Four brothers, Sydney, Donald, Eric and Roy, attended one school in Gloucester; "The King's School" is its name. It is close to the Cathedral. Mighty proud of it were all those who belonged to it. The two eldest of the brothers got to Oxford from it and the youngest had hopes that way too. So, quite naturally, the boys were at daggers drawn with the scholars of the other schools in the city: The Crypt, Sir Thomas Riches and the Technical School. Rivalry is quite common in such circumstances. Boys find it hard to be objective so, rather as Nathanael could not imagine anything good coming out of Nazareth, the thought of leaving Kings and descending, yes descending to one of the others was inconceivable for the youngest.

Why leave? It is a sad story but one which, it is good to report. It has been completely reversed in these days. Now, what is a thriving, growing, busy and effective school was then in distressing and almost terminal decline. The decline struck Roy just about the time that secondary education should have been dealing with him. The King's had to become a preparatory school. Oh Shame!

There is no doubt now that the Crypt and Sir Tommy's or the Technical school, for that matter, would have dealt with him excellently, for those schools certainly gave good teaching to those who also had to leave at that time. But at that time such a move was beyond all consideration.

Roy's distress was severe. He was almost in a state of shock. He turned hopefully to *Hotspur*, *Rover* and such like; boys' comics of those days and very compelling reading. He had absorbed *Billy Bunter*, and that's no mean feat. He considered the fine life of a legendary boarding school to be the only possible alternative. Being inconsolable about King's he asked and begged to be sent away to school. I am not sure how this was managed. Canon Maynard Smith of the Cathedral is known to have had a deep hand in it. Parental sacrifice helped to make it possible aided by the generosity of Canon Robert Harwood, then the vicar of St. Mark's Church Gloucester. One of the Woodard schools, Ellesmere, found a vacant place, a desk, a bed and a welcome.

So it was that on one cold January day,

Ellesmere found itself invaded by two new boys. Roy and a lone German lad Ivor, was that his name? He had met suffering of a sort Roy would never experience. He was brave. Such was not the case of the boy from Gloucester. He had been very much aware of his loneliness as he stood beneath the upraised statue of St. Oswald, King and Martyr, waving towards a slowly departing little black car taking his parents back home. The wide straight drive led between some tall dark trees to the College gates, out into the field and round a bluff which hid them from sight. He would be eighteen before they came again. But weep not; St Oswald did not rule over a prison, the 13 year old would return home every holiday.

Meanwhile, after a few days, the strangeness of the new environment overwhelmed him. No one hit him or attacked him but inside, there was a chilling pain with the double embarrassment of being entirely responsible for this pain. He was homesick. He could not tell anyone about it and he wept. Then he had to write cheerfully home. There they could certainly read between the lines. They sent regular encouraging letters back to him.

Years later his mother spoke of her tears when she had waved farewell at the College gates. Parting from loved ones, especially parents is not a sweet sorrow at all, it can be bitter at the time, even if there is laughter later. There *is* laughter later, there is pain and there is excitement and other odd things as well, as you will find if you care to follow the track of these mere memories.

Where From?

When boys meet - their names and nicknames introduce their persons. Interest may develop between them as to their homes, what games they play, what comics they read, and the quality of their faces or the oddity of their physique become notable.

In the first term all the new boys are new together, they have a fellowship of strangeness to experience, so they give some support to each other as they settle down. By the time the second term begins they know the ropes, they know each other, they have picked out particular friends and are no longer new to the system.

Watch therefore these two new boys who join the school in the second term; the cold dark, January term. One of them, Roy, has had Christmas at home with all its joys, surrounded by those he knows and in the warmth of their love. Now encased in a new uniform, wandering unknown corridors, facing a host of unknown boys, all apparently older than he is and seemingly completely at home amongst the vastness of the buildings.

He enters the mighty darkened dining Hall for his first evening meal. His place is at the bottom end of the bottom table in the block of tables that delineate his "House" of about sixty boys. To say he is much overawed hardly meets the feeling, but it must do. The boy at the top of the table, one term old and feeling the weight of his great superiority seeks a laugh at the expense of the new boy. He also seeks to impress the others so he calls out down the table "And what bin do you come from?" Roy is taken aback by this question as he never regarded his home or his former school as being in the least 'bin' like. However, attempting to turn the awaiting and giggling expectancy of his future friends to some advantage and being a humble mortal and not wishing to claim a higher place than he ought, replied,

"Number Two." Well there was laughter, scornful laughter and some appreciative laughter. The table settled down to the serious business of eating.

Roy never made real friends with his first tormentor, which is a pity. A scornful challenge is not a helpful way to build a relationship. At that time he felt as if he could have been some scrap from the depths of a very doubtful and undistinguished canister, very much out of place. But go on a couple of terms and the newness has gone. School becomes a familiar place, friendships are formed. It is nearly home for home. Bins have nothing to do with it.

Antique?

It is to be found in the wardrobe. It had been
there a long time, as indeed most of the stuff
hanging there. It must have been there from
school days doing its job patiently,
effectively, without fail. Yes it is a clothes
hanger, one of the wooden sort. Hardly an
important antique to ruffle the courts of
Christies, even if it is well over fifty years
old. So what is so memorable about it? It has
the number 27 scratched and inked upon it.
Again so what? That number is a boy's
school number by which every document,
every item of clothing, each shoe, sock, and
book is marked. The only unmarked item is
the owner of the number. Boys were not then
tattooed with their school number, it might
have happened since but others must tell of
that.

This new boy was a little surprised. It was
such a small number. He had been informed
about it during that Christmas holiday.
Having been given to understand there were
some hundreds of boys in the school,
whatever had happened to the others, 28 and
onwards, had they all been spirited away by

some wicked teacher? Of course you are right! It just happened to be a free number on the files formerly belonging to one of the older boys who had recently left the school. How many 27s have there been in the 150 years of the life of the school? Average stay per boy, say 5 years? 30 lads in all and of those probably only 10 living now. What a select bunch! Greetings to whomsoever is number 27 today. Many years later, when making up a parable about a family called the Lightfoots, 27 Heavenview Road came to mind. Yes it has always been a special number. One to be recommended.

First Letter

Food glorious food! Oliver Twist is not unique. Never has there been a boy's stomach that does not ache for good food. Difficult it is indeed for cooks, Mums, or chefs to pump sufficient edible material into the gaping voids that lurk beneath the open mouths of the ravenous chicks called boys.

Now our Sunday dinners at home, indeed all our dinners at home were very satisfying. Mother could cook meat fit to grace a banquet. Not so the Sunday dinner at school. There was something about the meat and gravy, its smell and appearance that did not ring true. Yes, a slice of roast beef it used to be, rather thin, about the thickness of the tongue of a leather shoe. In shape roundish, as big as a small hand, in colour, black going to grey at the edges which curled up threateningly, cracked and ready to splinter. This floated in a brown ink which was called gravy. Two veg' went with it, but not very well, having been excessively well cooked. Of course in my first letter home I tried to describe my horror at the meal but all I could manage then was, "We had dinner of beef and

gravy, two veg. with custard and apple pie."
Mum was so pleased to know I was being
properly fed, just as at home .Well maybe it
was good that she was happy about it but my
stomach looked eagerly beyond the endless
weeks of term to a homecoming dinner
worthy of the name.

Tut. TUT. Language

I hear, from other schools, that new boys could be badly treated. This was not so in my experience. We were rough with each other from time to time but no bully boy tactics were practised. One organised event was, however, scary.

Every new boy in the junior dorm' had to sing, recite a poem or do other such display of wit, standing on one of the lockers, which separated each bed space, and this in the presence of the Housemaster. He was encouraging, although some of the boys were justifiably ribald in their comments, even if every attempt was clapped at the end. I had managed to learn the ditty about the Tower of London with poor Anne Boleyn walking with " 'er 'ead tucked underneath 'er arm". Now you must know that I was "properly" brought up. Thus to sing "Bloody Tower " was at that time beyond my courage. Therefore then, and probably for the first and only time in history, the whole song was produced without the offending word. "She walked - the - Tower" rang round the dormitory in my tremulant treble reducing Gracey - that was our housemaster, Mr Field, to a burst of hysterics. I didn't realise what he found so funny at the time but was pleased to have got through the ordeal with his apparent approval. I know I had a built in ignorance about bad language. In the Armed Forces later I had to look up in a dictionary the more regularly used adjectives spoken by my comrades. I still think their conversations would have been better without the endless repetition of boring four letter words, after all I had missed out one six letter word without losing a laughing response.

Trial

For two weeks new boys are permitted to explore the school. Staircases, normally out of bounds, corridors and odd rooms bore no hazards. No punishment for the infringement of rules would be given BUT, after those cheerful, free and easy days, the full force of the law would be applied, after due warning. So, by the middle of the first term, young lads fell inevitably into troubles of various sorts.

Take running in the corridors for example. Very sensibly, running, as it was a danger to life and limb, was forbidden. You may think that it is a lot of fuss about nothing, until you consider the thirty or so boys charging headlong to thirty others speeding towards them in a narrow corridor. There would ensue a clash of the Titans as two irresistible forces meet. An explosion of nuclear force results. So running down corridors is forbidden.

In my first terms a horrendous, psychological method of punishment was in force. It happened like this. Suppose I darted down said forbidden passage and was caught hotfoot by some House Prefect on say a

Monday. I mean why not run on Monday? Well instead of having some suitable penalty, like having to stand still for ten minutes or having some lines imposed, the offender, i.e. me, would be told to attend Prefects' Court. This would of course be held in the Library on Friday. Imagine spending the whole week wondering what horrific fate might be dealt out by such an august body of huge seniors. Can you see a line of timid youngsters the following Friday clinging to the wall outside the library, me halfway down the queue as my name begins with L? One by one called in. One by one emerging to tell of lines, tasks, even beatings to be given. Then, finally, me terrified.

"Enter! Stand there before that table."

Behind the table Purple clad School Prefects glare at the guilty. The House Prefect reports the offence.

"Well what have you to say about that?"

Silence.

"Nothing? Right! Guilty!"

They all nod.

"You have been accused and are guilty of running on the main corridor, so... (Here it comes - thoughts of thumb screws, thousands of lines to write, all future free moments to be spent pushing heavy rollers up and down the cricket pitch etc;)..''You must write... (inward sigh of relief).. one hundred times: "I must not run in the corridors."

Nod.

"Next".

Those lines were tedious but as you see I have remembered the rule fifty years later and the cruel days of anticipation.

I am glad to report that those courts only existed in my first year. It was really awful if the offence was noted on a Saturday. Just think, a whole week, including the weekend, wondering what impossible or horrible fate was in store. Those great and powerful Prefects had authority over life and limb, or so it felt. It really was a trial.

Drink Up

It's disgusting! Amongst many horrors can you name one worse than this? Boys, after evening prep', walking along the darkened main corridor. Silent, because to raise the voice in idle chatter outside the Head's study, the School Prefects rooms or the staff room is liable to bring down mighty wrath. Boys nevertheless speed along like mice for the night cap.

This is a mug of hot liquid and a biscuit available just outside the dining Hall. You notice 'hot liquid' that's the disgusting bit. How it was managed or by what art of wickedness was involved, none could fathom. It was called cocoa. No maker of that delight could recognise the brew. Never did it taste like this at home or in scout camp. Dark it was. Cow juice it never saw. Sour it was, sugar a stranger to it. Worse than all that it was burnt, yes carbonized with the flavour of soot. But Drink Up! Yes, Drink Up!

Surely we were training our taste buds to deal with the unknown nasty future when we might have to eat unmentionable objects to keep alive in the wartime. That must have been the reason. At no time in the forces, in foreign fields, in England or even in America or India did we face a more disgusting flavour. On the ladder of deliciousness it had not reached the first rung, indeed it had not surfaced from the compacted ashes on which that ladder stood. But it was hot or at least warm depending on one's place in the queue and that was its only virtue. The biscuit that went with it was fine. It did not matter what type of dry offering came along even if it was not all that dry for that matter. In comparison to what had to be drunk it took the biscuit.

Catch!

There is no doubt that Meynell House was blessed with good house masters. Naturally a member of that house would say nothing else, loyalty being what it is. To me Gracey was such a person even if his surname, Mr. Field, demanded such a nickname. A fine Chemistry teacher and a sympathetic caring house master.

He had one particular peculiarity which younger boys were warned of. He threw things about. The time came for our special evening treat. Something looked forward to with trepidation, an invitation to about six of us to Gracey's study for evening chocolate and cake before bed. Suitably washed, clothed in pyjamas and dressing gowns we filed into his room.

It was winter and so for the second time that term we were met with a blazing hot coal fire, very cheerful that was. The first time was the first night of the term, when the dormitory fire was lit, and that was its only time. So we sat in very comfy chairs toasting our toes. Gracey chatted about this and that and told the odd joke which we dutifully enjoyed. Then came the dreaded test. This was the days before spinning discs. He spun china plates at us. One by one they came at us. We often had butter fingers, but, with the accuracy of a Greek discus athlete, his unerring aim got them into our laps.

"Good," he would say when the delivery was over "No need to charge and punish anyone for breakages."

Then would follow delicious slices of cake and mugs of sweet hot chocolate, which he did not throw at us.

Yes those were good evenings, graced by a kindly host whom we respected and yes for whom we had much affection. We trusted him. He never shamed us before each other. I found him a real encourager.

White Faces

I must not give the impression that life at College was always grim, it was actually interesting, we had many good teachers, there was laughter and mutual sympathy. But grim things did happen. The one I now retell was just one event, on one day, in my five years stay. It happened like this.

A senior boy ran away from school, absconded, played truant. He was not just off for an afternoon he made a meal of it and was off for days. He being a senior and I being at the time a very junior junior all we got were rumours of his wild adventure. Eventually he was brought back by the police, if I recall properly, who had spent hours looking for him over a wide area.

That evening all the senior boys - that is nearly everyone but us were called into the Big School. Punishment. Public Punishment was to be meted out. We were thrilled. We were also angry at being excluded. Cross at being just too young. It was no good hovering about the doors of the Big School where the rest of the College were assembled. We had no chance of being admitted or hearing anything. So we waited in distant recesses as the Head walked, no, stalked by, be-gowned and obviously very, very angry. We shrank further into invisibility as he passed and then cautiously, like inquisitive hamsters crept out to await the return of the witnesses to the beating which would surely be given.

Have you ever seen whitewashed skin? I have. It was half an hour later that we saw the white tense faces of silent seniors, all with wide startled eyes. They brooked no questions. Something indeed truly awful must have happened. We got the gory details later and shared the shock, although second hand.

Apparently, so we were told, the parents of the absconder had requested the Head to deal out massive punishment. This consisted of a harsh beating of twelve strokes of the cane on his bare behind to be witnessed by the school. The Head was a very big man, very strong of arm and character. Maybe those who let us into the secret of the punishment added to its telling but when I said "gory details" earlier it was no mistake. Blood indeed flowed. It took some time before the event retreated into the back of our minds. The senior in question was regarded by us as something of a hero and yet also something of a chump. We did not understand the reason for his absconding. However, no one, yes this is true, no one ever again ran away from school during my time there. Maybe none of us ever wanted to be the cause of so many white faces?

In and Out

"You are never to leave the College grounds without permission." That was one of the rules. Quite sensible, I suppose, for the staff had responsibility for our welfare and could hardly look after us if we weren't there. However, on Sunday afternoons it all went into reverse. "On Sunday afternoons you will not be on the school premises. You will go for a walk unless it is pouring with rain." I never realised the illogicality of these contradictory orders until now.

So, come Sunday, walk we did, togged up with cap and overcoat in winter. Lightly clad on more balmy days. Two or three pals together. Now and then we might pass odd teachers being good and other members of the school on the same task, but we tended to ignore them and be ignored by them. This mutual blindness helped us to enjoy the countryside and it was enjoyable. Nearby the canal system presented ideal conditions for interesting strolls but never a boat did we see, for they did not exist in those decaying days of the canals.

The canal took us, in one direction, high above the fields and in another into a long tunnel. To walk along that towpath was a thrill. The dark water beneath our feet, the inky black wet walls, the echo of footsteps, the drip of doom, the raised voices in high laughter to cloak hidden fears and the relief of daylight as we emerged unscathed like heroes at the further end. Beyond that came another delight, which actually entered my nightmare life. The canal gently curved round the edge of Black Mere, well named because it was not large but almost completely surrounded by high and, in winter, gnarled forest trees. The towpath has the canal on one side and the dark waters of the Mere on the other. The brooding waters obviously contained slimy leviathans with grasping tentacles ready to trip the careless boy and drag him into the muddy depths. I can't remember staying long there even in bright sunlight. However, the sound of birds, the really majestic trees and the quietness of the waters made that walk a real treat.

It was the friends that made those times such

a joy, Slab, Peter and others. We chatted about school life, the war, our families, books, stories, fantasies, fictions and facts. Those afternoons were good for us even if, being naturally reluctant, we begrudged the effort of going out. Well, it was good to come back in and have tea.

The Long and Short of it

No place here for those whose desire, on winter afternoons, was a cosy laze round the friendly radiators. Run or Games. Games or Run. That is the order. No escape. Ah! Yes! Run. Jog. Trot or a bit of both. The sooner it was over the better then the radiators could resume their warm companionship. This was all very well later in the term when it was not all that painful BUT the first expedition out onto the lanes, that circumnavigate the college grounds, could be agony.

Out through the main gate, turn left, as if running into the local town, always "out of bounds" that was, so left again between hedge rows and fields until at last the entrance to the lower playing fields come in sight. A good sight that. Then trot, run, walk or stagger up the final slope and so back into the changing rooms for a shower. Come rain or shine, snow, ice or wind young mortals brave the elements with pounding feet and labouring breath. It was, however, the muscles that took the strain. They informed us on rising next day, that they were cross, very cross. After the soft sweet holidays on good food, parties, with little or no exercise to speak of, said muscles, even after the Short Grind's exertions, grumbled out loud. We could hardly stand, hardly move at all, to be accurate, but move we did to breakfast. The stomach took control. Leg ache we could face, stomach ache certainly not and anyway other powers would turn us out of bed if that was not accomplished voluntarily.

There were a few of us who turned right outside the main gate on the first run, to tackle the Long Grind, about three times further than its short brother. Were there ever any that took both Grinds in their stride? Not me, I assure you. They must have been exceptional athletes or exceptionally stupid. Take your choice. For me the Short Grind was always too long for a first run.

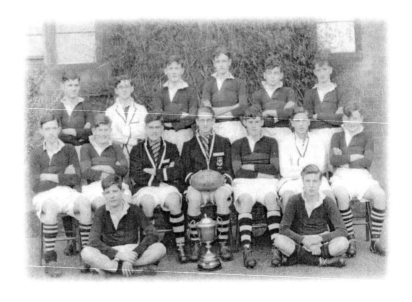

P.T. (Physical Training)

It may have been frosty, cold it often was, but as it was not raining, ten minutes of P.T. were nipped into the start of break at the end of the first session of morning lessons at 11 o'clock. "Yes you will change into gym shorts, vest and shoes and you will enjoy the fresh air even if you a covered with goose pimples." Compulsion was required to get us outside, little flocks of shivering sheep scattered over the roadways around the buildings. Senior and Junior members of each of the four "Houses." No encouragement was needed as we proceeded to jump up and down, swing arms about, bend and stretch at the sound of a commanding voice. Physical Jerks it really was. I suppose it was quite good for us growing lads. But when the wind was of that lazy biting variety which didn't bother to go round you, our puny frames longed for rain.

When it rained P.T. was cancelled. Then we had a full half hour break all to ourselves. Bliss. Even time to visit the Tuck Shop. The rain, as one might expect always stopped at ten minutes to eleven or started at about half past the hour. I doubt in all my years of suffering P.T. that we escaped the drill more than a dozen times. No wonder we were such fine, upstanding specimens of humanity.

There were competitions, later in the year, with the carrot of a fine silver cup to be won for the House. All teams were eager to win that. The timing of the drill was exact, the flow of movement perfect, and each one knowing the next exercise so that no commands were necessary. When we won, it seemed all those ten minute stretches of agony were worthwhile. It is amazing how a silver cup can change the attitude and even make those who came second or third inordinately proud of their prowess in P.T.

Sun worship

Sad the man who has never lent back on a grassy bank in the summer sunshine to feel the glorious warmth of the heavenly furnace penetrate right through to the backbone. The terrace slopes below the back quod' are ideal for this purpose. Surely they are still in use? It must have been the summer term of 1940, an idyllic term for cricket and tennis and for lazing about, (but for the mighty war reaching its most critical stage and the Battle of Britain in progress). The sun shone in the clearest of blue skies day after day.

We got used to facing the sun and chatting dreamily to each other about the impossible news. Yet something odd happened around the sun one afternoon. Close to the sun, yet not too close, there appeared a circle of mist like a halo. Gradually it widened its diameter, moving steadily across the sky, a band of white against the pale blue of a vast cloudless sky. The band did not seem to thicken or widen, it just grew towards the horizon. We had to leave for late lessons long before the horizon was reached. What was it? A sign? Angels coming to earth? A white circular cloud bow of promise? There was no rain in that sky. It certainly heralded many disasters and terrific victories in the air battles.

Maybe there is some scientific explanation, but to us it was odd in an odd sky at an oddly significant time. But then, we were odd boys anyway.

Boanerges

Even Jesus gave people nicknames. John and James he called "Boanerges" (Sons of Thunder). Simon became "Cephas", Peter the "Rock Man". We only followed his example. Of "Slab Ellerton" I will tell later. My pals had a job with me as I had no distinctive physical features. However, both they and I were brought up on the adventures of the radio series "Toy Town." As my surname is Lambert, Larry the Lamb, who was after all the hero of the series, came to mind. "Larry" I became. It was a pleasant one to own all my school life.

Teachers suffer from nicknames. Dear old Mr Lush. He was one of those brave retired schoolmasters who drafted himself back into the task of teaching Physics when war service carried off our teachers. He was certainly a good teacher, thrilled with physics but not so very thrilled with boys to whom the subject was a problem or even impossible. We called him "Sniffer Lush" because he constantly sniffed.
"Now boy, what are you doing? *Sniff.*"

In addition he had two pairs of glasses. The first was always perched on his nose. Through these he was able to see our often puzzled faces, but when it came for him to look at his notes or our scribble, he had to insert another pair, without ear pieces, behind his long-distance specs. Therefore when holding his book in one hand and trying to catch our attention with some mystery of physics he would look at the book through them both and then with the second pair upraised would glance at us. "Now boy, *sniff*, (right hand and second glasses elevated) page 23 bottom line, (second pair slotted in behind the first and right hand free) read it out loud boy. *Sniff*." And so the up and down of the glasses would emphasise some point all through the lesson, each elevation marked by "*sniff*" and sometimes "*sniff, sniff.*"

Nevertheless, he got me a distinction in the national exams. He may not have been a Boanerges but he urged us to excel.

Not Fair

You must know that young boys do have a highly tuned sense of justice. They are not alone in this, even young girls are known to proclaim with vigour if some such situation is just "not fair."

The situation I mention is personal. It has to do with an English essay. Not, you might suppose, a very likely field for a miscarriage of justice. The sense of unfairness is however with me still, even although I cannot remember the person responsible. The situation concerns the setting of a task, such as any English teacher might demand from his class. This task was for us to write an imaginative short essay on the theme of "At Night." I worked at that.

In the library I found a Roget's Thesaurus - what a wonderful aid that is to essay writing. I must have spent hours with it seeking what I thought were just the right words. My "At Night" concerned moonlight slanting through the tall reeds that skirted a still pond. I was very pleased with the result and enjoyed it. It was a real painting in words and all my own work. It, with all the other attempts by the class, were duly handed in and a day or so later returned to us. When I saw the mark of 5 out of 10 I was not pleased, I always got that mark. I really thought a higher than usual award was justified. So, bold as I could be I asked the master why my mark was so low. "Because," said he, "You could not and did not write that essay. You got it from some library book."

"UNFAIR!" screamed my heart.

"I did write it," said I, "It was all my own work," said I, with lower lip all of a tremble. "I don't believe you, but I'll give you 7 out of 10 just in case."

I forgive that man now but his words and actions made a lasting impression on me. Ever after I realised that "they" did not really trust me or my word! It was unnerving to be so accused of what was in effect cheating and lying. A terrible thing for a boy and so unfair.

Much later, when coming to study those who make judgements about who did or who did not write the Epistles in the New Testament, I knew that it is quite possible to write out of character and use words far beyond the usual personal vocabulary of the writer. As a result I give St Paul 10 out of 10 for all the Epistles that claim to be written by him and St. Peter likewise. I do apologise to whatever unknown writer scholars may have penned 2 Peter, but you see, I'm not going to be unfair to St. Peter or doubt his authorship. I know just what it feels like!

Blenki

Might the name of a teacher have some bearing on the ability of a boy to learn his lessons? It cannot just be a case of irresistible ignorance, or can it?

Take French for example. The French teacher was most unfortunate. Blenkinsopp is not a formidable name. It does not inspire terror nor even a mild attack of anticipation. In fact, a smile, a chuckle or even a laugh is surely permissible? We must apologise to all those who are landed with that name who might be very active, bold and brave. Our Blenki, to which his name was reduced was, however, none of these. At least in my eyes. Mind you in retrospect he must have been all of these to have had the courage to deal with the impossible likes of yours truly. I was indeed a hopeless case. My grasp of any foreign language was and is so slippery it would drive any teacher to distraction. The only command I recall was his method of starting us off on some language test which he wanted us to complete in a particular time. Very good for those who knew the answers. Not me. Anyway he would tell us, "When I say begin,

commence. Start." And start we did.
Scribbling down all the wrong answers or just
looking at the questions with dull
bewilderment. French needs more that lists to
learn and vocabularies to memorise and very
irregular, or regular verbs, for that matter, to
master. Blenki, you did your best, but French
to me remained blinking impossible.

Frayling

Much maligned he was. Tended to spray those who were near him as he talked, but apart from that, a musical genius. What didn't he know about musical instruments, orchestras and symphonies? He was a very score of information. The music school resounded to his teaching and the great names of classical composition had to be learnt. Henry Hall was not enough. "*Red sails in the sunset*" and "*Hold your hand out naughty boy*" were beyond the pale. He ruled the music school and chapel. His inspiration even made us sing madrigals with the "*Fa la la!*" or gather to deal with "*Blest Pair of Sirens*" most suitable for wartime. The choir sang beautifully, often stunning me with anthems of glory. One anthem I have never heard anywhere else but was sung sometime each year was "*Remember now thy Creator in the days of thy youth*". It began with the most scary bass, joined later with the trebles soaring up with "*and one shall rise up with the sound of a bird and all the daughters of music be brought low*".

It was the chapel organ which proved to be

his forté. He was accurate and sensitive and adventurous on it. You could not imagine a more inconsiderable personage producing such a gigantic range of awesome and beautifully touching sound on that fine machine. Each Sunday night he faithfully placed on the chapel board the title of his after service voluntary. His choice was wide. Some stayed behind to listen and as there was always a little time before the evening meal, I normally remained in my seat. Why leave when an unknown treat was there for us to hear? My education in music and the thrill of the sound of the organ pipes began then and has never ended. My appreciation of the many organists I have known since began with Mr Frayling, whose dancing feet made the great pipes sound and never a false note did I hear from his fingers.

Beyond Endeavour

It was, I am sorry to say, all Greek to me. K. G. Todd, our great Latin master, struggled with us, and with me in particular.

"Amo, amas, amat," I could manage, but the love of the subject never grasped me and the pluperfect and subjunctives floored me, it might just as well have been Greek. He tried kindly to help us scan Latin verse with an English ditty, to give us the Rhythm. I liked that.

"Down in a deep dark well sat an old man chewing a beanstalk.

Out of his mouth he spat.

Bits of a.

Dirty old hat. "

But I still could not get my tongue round the Latin words. However, it was not for want of trying. I worked at it all right but never caught the charm of the language. It was complicated beyond my reasoning and far outstripped the capacity of my memory banks. Mark you, I enjoyed the stories. The myths and history of ancient Rome were a feast for my ravenous imagination.

I was a great disappointment to Mr Todd. He tried his best, gently encouraging or loudly frightening as seemed best for him. Neither method worked. However, I admired him very much and mostly because he quoted Winston Churchill on every possible occasion.

"Never in the history of human endeavour" was said with radio accuracy, perfect intonation, and guttural growls all in a slightly tipsy rhythm. K. G. Todd used these words to condemn the results of our exercises or the extraordinary times when someone or maybe a few got everything right. This entertainment was often enthralling especially as Winston, as we all thought, was undoubtedly the best possible person to copy. In due time many of us also learnt to copy him, K.G.T or Winston. They were all the same to us! This was an accomplishment which has been my party piece many times since, so Latin lessons were not a complete waste of time.

Along with Latin, our master of the craft had a fine choice of nicknames for us. My special friend, along with Peter Brown, was Maurice Ellerton. He was of large frame but had a withered leg which made him stomp about with a dignified limp. To see him running courageously was both breath-taking and frightening as well. It was impossible for him to swerve or stop suddenly, so he would just carry on and pity anyone in his path. K.G.T. always called him "*Monumental Slab*". We took this as a sign of great honour. He was a good Latin scholar, so monuments were in keeping with his stature, both physical and intellectual. We called him "Slab". Indeed "Slab" Ellerton is how I remember him now with great pleasure and respect.

The quality of our handwriting caused many an exasperated shout. Mr. Todd would accuse some boy of writing with a *Mashie Niblick*. What frightful thing this could be was beyond me at the time. I certainly could not spell it. I had never had one as far as I knew and took special precautions with my untidy hand to avoid such a horrible accusation. It was many years later that I realised the offending writing implement was a golf club. I then understood the implication of messiness on a page of slipshod translation, which also fell short in legibility.

I am so glad someone translated the Latin stories into English. I will always be thankful for that, but please never ask *me* to translate anything from English into Latin, even Winston Churchill found that beyond human endeavour.

Tick-Tock

It is an honour to be a server in the Chapel.
This was especially so in the early mornings
to serve at the Holy Communions with Syd
Sharpe the Chaplain. It was a skill I learnt as
soon as I was of an age to be included in the
ranks of servers at the altar.

On Sundays there was no problem as the
whole school was awake together and servers
just had to get to Chapel a little earlier than
others, but on weekdays it was a different
matter. Normally it was only the rising bell
that could get my eyes prised open and so
drag reluctant feet to the floor. What to do
about waking up over half an hour earlier in
order to be in time for the early service? Syd
had the answer.
"Borrow my alarum clock."
So it was duly borrowed.

Its tick was terrific, its bell better than a
speeded up Big Ben, yes, a hundred times as
fast. Therefore in order to keep in fellowship
with the rest of the dorm' it had to be suitably
doused. Would the locker do? No, that just
acted like a large sounding board, a drum

sending out an African message to everyone. Where to put it? Under the pillow? Yes that was the only place. The dorm' was saved. My sleep was not. Tick-Tock in the ear, from about three inches away, only slightly muffled by the fluff of the pillow. All through the night a disturbed, distracted, hesitant slumber. Dreams of being chased by bell towers or shot by machine guns. Finally, when at last exhausted and fast asleep, the alarum would go. All the fire bells and police sirens together are not to be compared with an angry alert alarum clock under a sleeper's head. That head shot up vertically followed by shoulders and chest, hands meanwhile desperately seeking the plunger to stop the racket. No one stirred. The dorm' was saved. I still had friends. Does the good Lord take account of His suffering servants i.e., me? I couldn't tell Syd.

Ice

Have you ever been cold? What a silly
question, of course you have! One year the
cold was very severe. It had various
interesting effects. For example our basic
human needs were met conveniently in the
two lines of toilet pots in brick seating
cubicles, opening into the open air against a
brick wall, without doors on any of them of
course. No one dawdled much over that
necessity in winter months, but when the frost
set in, everything froze solid, the toilet pots
included. Then the pressure on the very
scanty indoor toilets was immense! It was
such a winter. Weeks of very hard frost.
Many queues with lads in great need and very
grumbly at the tardy ones.

No rugby. No hockey. The ground was far too
dangerous. What to do? Well the Meres were
also frozen over, ice a foot or so thick.
Beautiful to behold. Ellesmere itself was out
of bounds as always, but Black Mere, White
Mere and Kettle Mere were available. It must
have been the whole school which skidded,
slipped and fell about on the ice of White
Mere. Snowballs zipped about all over the

place, often in my direction. The very few who had skates showed off alarmingly, while the rest of us spent most of the time spread-eagled wondering that water could really be that hard. Yes great fun.

One of the younger teachers caused a minor sensation by encouraging some bare foot walking in the snow. The cold numbed the feet, yet the snow caused them to tingle. "Absolutely delicious" said the converts. As for me, the friendly radiators were too encouraging to leave for some exquisite chilly sensation. I think it was the same teacher who went over the top with raw carrot. Well there are people like that who make something out of nothing, yet carrots instead of sweets was not so bad an idea . I think he converted many of us into happy rabbits at the time.

Ice and snow changes more than the scenery. You should have seen the telegraph wires weighed down into drooping curves by inch thick ice and heard them clanking in the wind. That is a rare treat these days now wires are nearly always underground.

When next it gets really cold and ice forms on roads and ponds please remember those frozen pots and have compassion on those caught short.

Skiing

Never had a chance to Ski. Europe? Out of bounds by order of some chap called Adolf. We didn't like him. Snow fell on the Highlands of Scotland but that was of no use to us. There developed, however, a skill akin to skiing on the snow slopes. This is "staircase slipping," a skill I advocate for any who happen to be within reach of a stone staircase with worn treads. This skill does not involve a moving staircase, like an elevator, but is an art, learnt fairly quickly by lads with quick feet.

The object of the sport is to descend the stone steps from the upper to the lower floors with an ankle movement equivalent to the flip of the wrist. In this the sole of the foot rests but the fraction of a moment on the nose of each stone step, not touching or pausing on the tread. It is a very speedy and moderately dangerous mode of descent, therefore great fun and in constant use.

The steps had been considerably worn when I came along, so I very soon became expert. It was a terrible disappointment to return after some summer holiday to find that each worn step had been reinforced with granite chipping concrete. It was a setback we never really were able to overcome but I have often used the technique on hillsides and other staircases. I really feel the sport should be given some Olympic accreditation, it is certainly speedy and demands much skill.

The stairs in question have no banisters. This was probably a deliberate policy for a boys' school. Had they been present they would certainly have become slides given half a chance. There was nothing to hang onto as speedy students swept round the 180° turn half way down the staircase. The brick walls at this point have received a high polish, like fine marble, by the grasp of thousands of boys nipping round the corner. How many hands do you ask? One could work it out approximately. 150 years x 14 weeks x 3 terms x 7 days each week. And about 120 boys descending for breakfast, for morning lessons after break, before lunch, for tea, for evening classes in the winter or afternoon classes in the summer and for night preparation work. That is x 8. I do not multiply by two for the two hands each boy presumably possesses as only the left hand could possibly be used on the turn but according to my calculations that comes to 42,336,000 hands. No wonder the polished bricks shine so much. Is that how Michelangelo got all his lovely statues polished? Did he employ all the grubby urchins of Rome to rub their unwashed hands on his work? I don't know, but that technique has certainly had good effect on the walls of the brick staircases.

Imagination?

Well it could be called that. It was wartime so the poor cook had little choice for our menu. We had enough to eat, but it was never very interesting. Boring could be the word. Did we grumble? Yes, a bit, but as no one could really do much about it we ate up and were thankful. There was rarely anything left on our crumbless plates.

Some among us experimented. I do not encourage anyone to repeat our mouth-watering attempts. We called each one a "re-cype" spelt to give it a French flavour for it tastes better that way. Such a re-cype would consist of a multiple bread sandwich in which layers of marmalade, jam, crumbled OXO cubes and a little mustard would be an "all sorts" bite, without butter of course. Having made it, it had to be eaten. It had an excitement about it, although our taste buds were somewhat amazed and dazed.

Liquid re-cypes were more difficult to concoct but if you would consider using cooking margarine instead of unobtainable milk for Ovaltine you will gather the depths to which we sank. Stewed damsons with saccharine as sweetener tasted metallic. Now you will understand why I always enjoy my meals in these days of such gigantic variety.

Darts

It is a great pity the large and lofty Dining Hall was burnt down a few years ago. Now-a-days the lower ceiling gives room for a further dormitory above, very sensible I'm sure but the pity about that fire goes beyond that. Not only were all the sports trophies of the school destroyed, silver cups for which we had worked so hard for our respective Houses, but the massive wooden beams held numerous secrets, sadly gone forever. These are secrets that could not be hidden in the present structure.

As soon as war got under way the boys on a roster basis had to take over such jobs as laying up the tables for meals, polishing the Chapel floor and polishing our own shoes. But this meant that we were often unobserved in the Dining Hall. Those were the days of push pens, iron nibs and ink bottles. Used gently, the nibs lasted quite a time, rough usage would break off the points leaving two very sharp prongs - ideal for sticking into things. Busy fingers could soon manufacture paper aerodynamic tail feathers to be held firm in the split rear end of the little barrel. I have no tally as to how many such darts hurled straight up during table laying duties remained fixed in the dark beams, time was available for such of us as that had Robin Hood tendencies to try and try again until our particular dart stuck firmly Home.

I had hoped, as an old man, to return one day and glance up to see if my dart was still in place. Sadly it must have suffered in the great fire. In such ways what we propose comes to nothing but it was still worth a try.

Grace

There we are standing silent at our benches, ready to leap over them en masse, sit and devour whatever food would be dished out from the senior or prefect at the head of the table. There we are waiting. In stalks all of the masters and the Head. They step up onto the raised dais where the long masters' table reaches across the top of the Hall. The Head comes to the centre, glances down the Hall and says the Grace.

Sometimes it was as bad as that. Just as if he had just said the word "Grace." He shortened the common Latin prayer of Benedictus; *"Benedicate per Iesum Christum Dominum nostrum."* Which I took to mean *"Blessings to and blessings through our Lord Jesus Christ."* However, there were times when either he was in a hurry or very cross or had just swallowed his Adam's Apple when he just seemed to say *"Benedic..."* as if someone had chopped off his head in the middle of a word. A Latin scholar will have to correct me in this. I am glad to say that the chaplain always spoke English and gave thanks to which we could genuinely respond a knowledgeable Amen. That was much more graceful.

The Crack of Doom

It only happened once in my experience. It happened in the Dining Hall during a busy meal. After Grace had been said the burst of chatter and the movement of benches heralded the distribution of food. Every eye watched as the senior boy divided, with mathematical accuracy, the tiny sliver of butter into the exact number sitting at table. We had about a finger nail of butter each for the meal. Rationed as it was to two ounces a week per person. Every meal had its exact division of all other foods, be they potatoes, tomatoes, fruit pie, sardines or even cabbage. We then settled down to consume everything available and chatted, laughed, grumbled, got angry, were cross with each other, hurt each other by words and generally behaved as you might expect ten or so boys of similar age to treat each other.

The noise level of nearly three hundred boys in full mouth is rather like the sound of a restless sea in a high wind. Breakers crash, rush the beach, scatter the pebbles, slither up the sand and claw it back, playing tricks on the stones. Endlessly this goes on. Now louder, now quieter. So in our every meal time the noise level ebbs and flows. Occasionally some important message had to be given by the Head. The little gong would ring to call for silence and a hissing hush and shush would gather into peace from the four corners of the Hall, to await the unexpected announcement. This speech would then play over a more restless volume of responsive tongues who would comment on the matter.

Once and only once, without gong, or hiss, or shush. Without knife scrape, bench groan, sliding plate or lone lost voice there was utter, complete, un-requested, absolute still silence. Masters at the top table were like statues of stone, the senior boys could have been in the midst of some deadly serious impossible exam and the juniors frozen with spoon raised and all lips sealed. *Uncanny* isn't strong enough. *Awesome* is more like it. A moment of cold clammy terror might approach the feeling of deathly quiet. There was once silence in heaven for half an hour, the biblical equivalent, our silence lasted ten seconds at the most, ears cocked like rabbits, eyes wide open like startled cheetahs and heads turning expectantly for some dynamic word. We began to take breath, for that had stopped too and as nothing but nothing was said, a hesitant murmur began to filter through the quietness to explode into a resounding "Whatever was that?" mixed with loud but nervous laughter. Were angels passing overhead? Had someone stood on our graves? Had something so awful happened in the world that it had touched everyone just like that? It was a shock to the system and we all wondered, pondering imponderables.

Tuck

I'm starving! That is not exactly correct but it is often thought between meals by boys and I expect girls also. Next to the Tuck shop is the Tuck Room stacked with hundreds of wooden, iron bound, boxes each one carefully locked. At certain times on certain days we were permitted to visit our treasure chests in which our precious jewels were stored. A real Aladdin's cave full of goodies.

In those boxes we hoarded food somehow gathered by kindly hearts and hands at home. Tins of fruit and ginger cakes, small tins of baked beans, biscuits, jam, Marmite and such like. Not sweets usually, for we had quite large rations of these from the tuck shop next door. This was the place where we got close to our distant parents and their edible concern for us.

Once, or was it twice a week, we could have our small tins of beans warmed up for high tea. What bliss! Even better if we had a friend to share it with and then share his later on. My birthday always fell in the summer term and some delicious cake would arrive on time, by post, to be shared with special friends and savoured over the following weeks. We had extras in the tuck shop like raw carrots, boxes of blackcurrant and apple pie. The aforementioned sweet ration kept us going between whiles. Yum Yum.

Piano Forte

Tum te-tum, tiddle tiddle tum te-tum etc; so the piano keys pounded out Chopin's Polonaise in A major. It was the Captain of School, Rogerson again. Every available free time he would mount the forbidden stage in the huge School Hall with its black wood block floor, long desks and high red brick walls. The stage was denied to all but those especially gifted few who were given permission to play the grand piano. He was greatly talented. He would play the whole piece, without a scrap of music, to my ear perfectly. As often as he began to play we would listen.

I can still hum most of the masterpiece. It was no wonder when at the end of a term, the music competition was held that he won the piano prize. Indeed the other boys although competent had no chance against such brilliance, indeed the judicator did not find a single point to comment on in his playing except to praise it as we all did.

I wonder if he continued playing? In my head I can still enjoy that music. Rogerson made

some dull and dismal days pleasurable even
in that daunting Big Hall.

Democracy

It was a good idea. Indeed it was a very good idea. It says something for the college that the Captain of School had such courage and faith to put it into effect and for the Head to permit the Great Idea. This idea was a reaction to the harsh disciplinary regimes which preceded it. No more punishments! No more caning! No trials! Every boy was put on his honour not to break school rules. Those who witnessed such tragic destruction of honour were to tell the offender to desist. No tale-telling! No reporting anyone!

Well we were very good. Yes we were! At least for a while. It was good to be freed from the oppression and fear some had experienced before Rogerson took over. I should think for a couple of terms all went well, but boys will behave like the fallen creatures we are, and a complete relaxation of discipline had the inevitable result you might well imagine.

The many continued to be oh very honourable indeed, but some fallen lads took advantage of the system to the discomfort of everybody and that was before the days of "Lord of the Flies". The number that "took advantage" increased until another kind of fear took over, the fear of feeling unsafe. The end of the summer term would herald another Captain of School; Baddely. I think we were all greatly relieved when he took charge of things. The pendulum swung back just a little. The regime reinstated punishments fit to meet the crime but without the harshness of former times. The cane would only be used when all else had failed to change behaviour. Indeed it was hardly used at all but was there as a last resort. We had admired Rogerson. Baddely was greatly respected.

The Walking Hero

It must have been the "floating foot" that first caught my attention. Let me explain. The way people walk can be most distinctive. Many, I agree, just move along without any distinction of note, but some with hesitant step or heavy tread or mincing feet, mark their way as if on tip toe. Boys are not noted for gentleness as they stride the world. The floating foot is therefore even more extraordinary among us.

There is undoubtedly a bit of hero worship in my noting this particular phenomena as the "boy" in question, very much a man in my eyes was very senior, indeed Captain of School, tall dignified, clever and a great sportsMAN, the capitals are deliberate, whereas I was a mere nothing. The way he moved showed the "floating foot" to perfection. It consisted of gliding, yes gliding is a fair description of the movement, as with long strides the leading foot is kept at least an inch off the ground with the sole completely horizontal and parallel to the floor. This gives the impression of never ever deigning to touch the earth. This was done without any sign of instability, serene and controlled would describe the motion. Of course what made it even grander was the full length purple gown worn, as was the tradition, only by the three School Prefects. School Captain, Prefect of Chapel and Prefect of Hall and then only after they had proved themselves worthy of such high honour. The manner in which each carried this noble garment impressed us with the character of the person so elevated.

Baddely was just grand as his tall frame swung the purple in rhythm with his stride, it emphasised the nature of his office and assured him of his place of authority which none of us would grudge him. His stride was captivating.

A Hero is liable to be copied. So many a younger lad tried to develop the same skill. None of us managed it, but not for want of trying. We thumped about, tottered along or swayed violently along the corridors. Thus it was our admiration grew for Baddely. For the only one who literally was above us, gave the distinct impression of being above the earth as well.

Such is hero worship.

Captain
John Bunt
VC.

V.C.

John Brunt was to me a senior of remarkable toughness. In all my school and University days I never saw the like of him again. He had many great friends among the older members of Meynell House and the rest of the College. We younger ones stood in awe of him. This was not because of his classroom brilliance but by his prowess on the sports field. He was full back in rugby, wicket keeper in cricket and in goal on the hockey field. Always he was the well nigh invincible, the last line of defence, a bulldog with indomitable courage. He revelled in saving the day. Many times only his bravery, as we saw it, stood in the way of a team's inevitable defeat. Built large, stocky and resilient, he was formidable. If, for example, it was impossible for him to get his hands or hockey stick up to a high ball before it crashed into the net, he would head it over the top of the bar and take no notice of the blow. Likewise, behind the stumps, quick with hands and feet, I can still hear the shock of the resounding thud as a super-fast delivery got through to his chest and he held it there without a qualm. However, it was as full back in rugby that he really needed watching. It was awesome. Brave indeed was anyone who tried to pass him. He took a try against his side as a personal insult. He threw his body wholeheartedly at the offender with the ball bringing him down.

Each year there was one particular match which the whole school was commanded to watch. This was the 1st XXV against the Staff. Now there were indeed some speedy, cunning and forceful members of Staff in the team and none so much as the Headmaster, a big man indeed and swift of foot. I am sure John was just waiting for the chance to bring the Head down. He got that chance. It seemed inevitable that the Staff were about to get a try and win hands down as the Head pounded towards the line. Then came John Brunt with a low tackle of such speed and force that seismologists in Tokyo felt the shock. It was a fair tackle but such was the impact that the Head was never able to play again and had finally to walk with a stick.

We said to each other when John Brunt left to join the Army that he would either get the V.C. or be killed. Gloriously and sadly both those prophecies were all too soon fulfilled.

It was absolutely in character for him to be in the midst of battle with bullets flying in all directions, sitting on a tank, directing operations against the enemy and turning a rout into a victory. That is how the story was told to me and it would be typical of him. I also heard that a snipers bullet killed him as he was later behind the lines having a cup of tea. If so, it was the only way they could get him. Of such men victory is made for it is not only on the playing fields of Eton that the mighty are prepared for battle.

Piggy

"BOY!!!!"

The word reverberated off the ivy-clad brick walls, piercing the lines of darkened windows. The silence was shattered, as if all the glass in the windows had taken flight and crashed onto the gravel below. The intense venom as of a thousand hissing snakes curled round the pointed bell tower and smashed into the ears of the lads transfixed on the main drive, as they shook at the scream of hate.

It was parade day. The Corps stood at the alert in dead straight rows in three petrified ranks, khaki clad in boots and putties. It might well have been 1914 but it was in fact 1941. The War was on. We were part of it. Getting ready for our manhood, fighting against an implacable foe. But here and now, Piggy, for that was our name for him, was our enemy. Our plump commander, whose bark was far worse than his bite, nevertheless had a bite to be feared, so his bark was terrifying. As that "BOY!" smashed round the three sides of the front quad, the boys, already at the alert, tense and stationary as statues in ancient Greece, heard the scream, high pitched and as piercing as a steam whistle continue;- "I can see the whites of your eyes moving"

They weren't mine. I knew that but it felt as if they were mine. Mine were already focused and fixed on one particular window sill in the Prep' school wing. That was to keep them still. It was best to concentrate like that, then head, hands, knees, backbone and toes were all absolutely still. Piggy wouldn't be able to see any movement in me not even with a microscope.

I suppose this all had to do with discipline, with self-control under difficulties, but I can't help thinking now that Piggy needed to show authority and enjoyed frightening us to death. Maybe I ought to be very grateful to him for when I did eventually join the Forces I had no difficulty with discipline nor drill. Indeed I was quite at home on the parade ground while others hardly knew their right hand from their left. So thank you Piggy. However, I still wonder if any of the boys really were looking about that day. Were you just out to scare us?

Marching on What?

Every cloud has a silver lining and some are so fluffy and comfortable that they are quite a treat. So it is with the O.T.C., (Officer Training Corps). Those who join the Corps - Oh yes, I must inform you how to pronounce that, for initially I thought it must sound like a dead body, a corpse. The better informed scornfully told me that the "ps" was silent and it should be pronounced "Cor" like unto "cor blimey" of Cockney fame. So, now being educated in this matter, back to the story.

Those who join the Corps, that is everybody old enough are equipped with boots, uniforms, caps and of course putties. Now this has nothing to do with the putty which a glazier uses to set window glass in place. No. Take a strip of khaki cloth about 4 inches wide and a yard or so long. Why? You may ask. Because a couple of these strips are putties. What to do with them? Make a neat roll and starting from the top of the boots roll the strip round and round the leg, up the leg to cover the lower part of the trousers below the knee and tie said strip in place. Tie firmly else when marching the putty had a tendency to come undone, to be trodden on joyfully by a joker of a friend. Do not, however, tie too firmly, else the blood flow to the feet would be hindered and sundry tingling and shooting pains would cause great dismay to the whole system. In case you have the wrong idea about the trousers, these were not full length or normal looking but more like "plus fours", that must be a golfing term surely? Anyway they were buttoned up just below the knee.

Well now, having got ourselves dressed, there were occasional "Field Days" away from College on Army exercise. Did we learn anything? Possibly. I was always credited as having been killed almost at once whenever I got to a practice battlefield and so very rarely could I fire the one blank round with which we were generously issued. We trudged here and there and were required to show officer qualities of leadership. I only did this once, I think. The so called "enemy" was on high ground in an invincible position. An odd blank was fired at them by one of us then, upending the rifle, the empty cartridge case was lodged in the end of the rifle barrel. Next we set the shoulder stock on the ground and fired the rifle with another blank. To our great joy the empty cartridge case ascended with great speed in a most convincing parabola up into the enemy encampment. Surely it must be a mortar shell turning head over heels. Surely this would give us the victory and lots of leadership qualities? It did neither. The umpires hadn't seen our brilliant use of arms and when they did hear of it we were severely reprimanded. "Someone might have been hurt or even killed" they said. We couldn't point out that there was a war on.

Was it Napoleon who told that victories were won in the stomach? If so we heartily agreed with his genius. At the end of every such field day we had an army meal and at the heart of that was an individual cold pork pie. We took it to be pork although the meat was black and gritty like walnuts to look at, but the pastry casing oozing with fat was absolutely delicious, I still find my mouth watering at the thought. After eating it we could have conquered any enemy that happened to be about and would certainly most cheerfully march anywhere upon that pork pie. It could almost be called a gold lining.

The Colours

Each year on a day carefully chosen to be hot and still the O.T.C. would be put through an inspection. This was an event dreaded by all. Some retired general with a cacophony of medals on his chest came to do the annual check-up. He wanted to see that this lot of budding officers were officer material and no mistake.

What did he check?
Could we *March*?
March we did.
Could we *Present Arms*?
Rather and *Slope* them too.
Could we *Eyes Right* and get ourselves into perfect formations?
Yes indeed.
Were we properly turned out?
Truly we were immaculate with buttons burnished like diamonds and boots polished to mirror the sunlight
But, more than this, could we stand absolutely still?

I am not sure what this compulsory inactivity was supposed to prove. It went on while the

General slowly, oh so slowly, walked between the rows of perspiring boys. I told you this would always be on a hot and sunny day. Now it happens on the parade grounds of Royalty and it certainly happened on our playing fields where the might of the O.T.C. was on display. It happened silently, it happened swiftly. Here and there gaps appeared in the ranks, like missing teeth in a budding child's mouth. It was as if a sniper in some distant tree was picking us off in as haphazard a manner. Boys just fell flat on their faces or flat on their backs. Some tottered off the field, drunken sailors dragging their rifles behind them like so many Mary's with lambs to heel. They were all fainting. But the General pursued his steady step regardless and we had to be regardless also.

"Stand still. Don't notice. Don't move a hand to help or even let an eyelid flutter."

It was a wonder any of us were left for the final march past when the General took the salute, band playing, arms swinging.
"A fine body of men" said the General, "Officers to a man."

Well we shall see about that when we come to enrol beneath "The Colours."

Winston Churchill

The radio in the corner of the Red's Day Room was the focus of attention. Alongside were various newspapers on a high reading desk.

Red being, by the way, the colour by which Meynell House was immediately recognised. The other three houses all had their specific colour. We read the papers more and more avidly as we got older and never missed the Nine O'clock news, if we could help it, especially as the War progressed.

It was a most exciting war. A War of massive defeats, the grim horror of the Fall of France and the capture of the whole of Europe was terrible indeed but heroic attacks and increasingly numerous victories in the air, on the sea and finally on the land caught our full attention. Add to that our seniors as they left, and some left in midterm, vanished into the forces and a few later paid short visits to the college resplendent in Uniform and very, very great in our eyes.

These were stirring days for us. In particular

the defeat and surrender of France and the miracle of the evacuation from Dunkirk were both shattering and inspiring in turn. However, it was Churchill who held us in the palm of his hand. We all listened to his every word. We knew that what he said was of personal importance. We would certainly have fought on the beaches, in the fields and in the streets for him. We were most willing to become members of "The Few" who later won the battle of Britain. At that time we chalked up the victories and losses of the tremendous fight in the air as if it was a life and death Test Match. Blood, sweat, tears, yes we were ready for that. To know we were part of these islands in their "Finest Hour" thrilled us and made us all grow in stature.

It was the radio that informed us of the progress of the war. Maps above the reading desk, with coloured pins, marked the movements of the front lines. But, as with most of the nation, we really did not know the awful brutal things happening on the continent, especially to the Jews and in the concentration camps. These were unthinkable, unknown, unimagined by us innocents. The shock of discovering just what the Nazi conquerors had done had to wait until the war was finally over, College was but a memory to me then.

I do remember our tense silent waiting on the words of Churchill. I see our solemn faces as he spelled out some awful facts and the smiles when he praised some magnificent achievement. I recall too that even in the darkest days with the situation quite impossible he gave hope and resolution. We just knew without doubt that victory would eventually be ours in spite of gigantic odds. It was the radio that communicated such word of certainty and through it we knew that Churchill had each one of us in mind as he spoke.

Detail from "The Triumph of the Innocents" –
William Holman Hunt – Displayed at Ellesmere
College during the war.

Culture

It arrived by surprise. We had Adolf to thank
for it. It happened in the Big Hall which was
and is indeed Big. Arched doorways lead into
various classrooms along one side, the arches
the other side in my day were bricked up. The
high stage, beneath a vast window, dominates
one end. The red brick walls, pierced only by
windows high up near the roof literally
walled us in. There is therefore a large
uninteresting area of red brick for us to
ponder on for inspiration as each night we sat
at long bench desks chewing pencils, doing
prep' in gruesome silence.

Naughty Adolf threatened. In response wise
art lovers and defenders of national treasures
and culture, in Liverpool's Walker Art
Gallery,   sought   temporary   safe
accommodation for pictures of world
renown. Whoever considered our school as
safe   accommodation   must   have   had
extraordinary faith or was incredibly naïve.

It is true that there was little reason for Adolf
especially to target our school, so in that they
were correct. But what about a few hundred

lively lads? Well I have to proudly inform you that their faith was completely justified. Not a book, stone, dart, or any other missile were ever cast at those pictures which suddenly arrived to decorate those huge blank walls. They became great friends. Pre-Raphaelite beauties amongst them. I shall never forget the massive "Triumph of the Innocents" with its delicious bubbles wafting the souls of the children to heavenly bliss and the others were delightful to study when we should have been deep into Maths or Latin. I promise myself a visit to the Walker Art Gallery one day. I wonder how many of those fine pictures I shall recall?

Dormitory Slumbers

Take twenty five or so boys, with the same number of beds separated by small wooden lockers and narrow rugs on bare boards, with a central gangway of dark lino and you have the makings of a dormitory. To complete the effect add a couple of large Railway posters and a framed picture. Our dorm had a wash place at one end with a number of bowls with cold taps to each. I know they were cold because when it came to my time to do my weekly shave I had to retire to the one hot tap in the corridor outside the bathroom. It never took us long to splash our faces and hands. The lofty walls were broken by tall windows and long curtains, suitably thick, blacking out all chances of light that might indicate our position to any prowling aircraft that happened to be about.

Up near the ceiling and running at well-spaced intervals right above the beds someone had fixed tin shields with dubious heraldic emblems emblazoned on each one. They may have had great significance to that said someone, but to me they were doubtful. We concocted their meanings, all wrong I expect. They were just there like many peaceful guardian angels, part of the furniture, watching over us as we knelt to pray before creeping between the cold sheets.

Sleeping is so natural that most of us fall into it readily, boys in particular, especially after a full day with an hour or so of sport or hectic squash, rugby, hockey, cricket, running or tennis to exercise the limbs. You may be astonished to hear that "lights out" usually resulted in complete silence after a moment or two. This was partly because we were naturally tired but also because it was dangerous to chatter after "lights out". There were painful penalties for disturbing the peace which we wished to avoid.

It was, however, wartime and so our peace was broken, now and then, by the invaders of our air space. We heard the drone, the deep pulsating thunder of German bombers passing nearby en route for Liverpool or some other target quite unknown to us. The "Air Raid" wail woke us up, but, as there were no air raid shelters for any of us, we just stayed in our beds, warm but waiting, keeping very quiet unless maybe "they" should hear us. No bombs came our way, anti-aircraft shells burst far away from us. We were never really frightened, although once or twice we did get a shock. The Germans were particularly urgent and persistent sometimes and then we were wide awake.

One night was different. Gigantic explosions, not very far away to our minds, shattered our complacency. The explosions set the shields high above our heads a-clanging and a-tingling and a-chipping and a-dancing on their lofty perches. I believe the bombers had scored some direct hits on some arms dumps near Oswestry. These set up massive, continuous thunder claps of fire, the light of which came through our blackout curtains, illuminating white faces. The blasts seemed to shake our tough buildings and our teeth. We were relieved some time later to note that the guardian angels resumed their gentle watching and were still.

Distant fires continued all night as we went back to sleep wondering what damage had been caused and grateful not to have been the target ourselves. The next day we were a little subdued and a little excited at the same time but normality soon returned as the serious matters of school life continued unabated. The war went back to sleep.

Sid Sharpe, Chaplain

To be Chaplain to a boys' school is a demanding business needing special sensitivity, the hide of a rhino and an acute sense of humour.

It is a calling of great opportunity for good, in witness to Jesus and the Gospel before teachers as well as the scholars. Sid showed these and other priestly virtues.

On one occasion he had the courage to sing his text, which brought down on his head the wrath of the Masters. But I never forgot it.
"I want to be happy but I can't be happy 'til I've made you happy too"
Well it may not be actual Scripture but it is jolly close to it. Sid taught those who were mature enough, to read the lessons in chapel with patience, encouragement and wit. We began to understand what we were reading and how important the passage was.

He led prayers with deep seriousness and faith. He challenged us to deal with the selfish and disobedient evils in us and, as one year we were at school over the Easter Feast, made Holy Week into a personal experience in which I for one came to a deeper trust and faith in Jesus as Saviour. He was ever a friend even when he had to rebuke a boy like me, now and then. When the war hit us we could no longer have evening prayers in the chapel, which was impossible to black out. That had been a great comfort to me in my first terms but morning chapel with its robust singing started the day with joy, seriousness and love. He had an especially good singing voice. To hear him take the part of Jesus in the "Story of the Cross" from the back of the original English Hymnal was formative in my understanding of Calvary and my response to it, for we had our part to play in that very long and moving hymn.

We had visiting preachers, bishops, missionaries, the general secretary of the "Waifs and Strays" (now called "The Children's Society") whom I happened to know through my home church, as well as the general secretary of the "Additional Curates Society". Each contributed in some way to the knowledge and life of the faith. One tall preacher had the habit of pushing his glasses up onto the top of his head, while he spoke to

us with some vigour, we were fascinated to
see them slowly moving forward to crash
down on his nose. He kept our 100%
attention, although of what he spoke I have
no idea.

The seriousness of the war was not ignored.
Sid placed a clear poster of its meaning on the
chapel board. A black swastika overprinted
with a red cross. It showed where the real
victory lay and where it would always be. We
talked together about the war and the
demands it would make. He had very positive
views on the necessity of Christians being
involved in the fight, whatever might be the
cost. He saw, more clearly than some of us,
the awful evil of Nazi dominance and its
cruelty to Europe and the world. So when the
time came to consider being called up for
service most of us volunteered willingly.

When the new Science Wing was finished
Sid became master-in-charge of the
dormitory above it. Others must tell of his
abilities there with the boys as I was well
established in Meynell by then. I understood
he was not above wielding the "slipper of
discipline" with considerable agility, when

necessary. I would like to know how others regarded his ministry but I for one am always grateful that my stay at Ellesmere was guided by his devotion to Jesus and straightforward down-to-earth teaching.

V. I. P.

Now here was someone really worth listening to!

He was every inch a Man, dressed in the very smart light blue uniform of an Officer in the R.A.F. with ring marks of high authority on his sleeves and a breastful of decorations of honour spread over his jacket. Verily a V.I.P. He was one of the "Few" by whose skill and determination the victory of the air came to us in the Battle of Britain.

The whole school was indeed honoured and sat enthralled to listen to his every word with breathless attention. He told a few stories of life as a fighter pilot and each tale encouraged us to follow his example. Indeed to follow his way to the stars and volunteer for the R.A.F. as soon as it became possible. He appealed to our loyalty, our English pride, and tried to install into us a lively hatred of the German oppressors. It was serious stuff, dramatic and dynamic. He touched, I would say, every heart in that Big School.

Immediately I, amongst others, set about

seeking entry as a volunteer into the R.A.F. as soon as 17th birthdays were accomplished. In due course a call came to go to London, to Adastral House itself, to be interviewed as a candidate for flying training. The train trip to London was exciting enough but to go to the very headquarters of the Royal Air Force was thrilling and quite daunting.

The questioning in the interview did not however endear me to the board. I did not seem to be at all the material the R.A.F. required. It seemed they really wanted to know that my hatred of the Germans was an acutely personal hate. They wished to see in me an earnest desire to kill as many Germans as I could. I'm afraid I got a low mark in the hate stakes. Then I was asked if I could swim. I said in all truth "No".
"And what is the use of the captain of a bomber crew shot down over the North Sea if he couldn't swim?" questioned one of the board. I indicated I had no intention of being shot down over the North Sea and anyway I wanted to be a fighter pilot. That ended my attempt to join the R.A.F.

A few months later I volunteered for the Fleet

Air Arm. I passed the medicals and was accepted for training as soon as I reached 18. The Navy didn't ask if I could swim and still I can only manage a width, provided I stay within my depth. My excessive enjoyment of the F.A.A. is another story.

FIRE!

What careless event caused the blaze I am not sure was ever discovered. Fire in a school is always a threat. The big buildings were carefully designed but there was a lot of wood about. Huge roofs and lots of furniture ready to combust, given half a chance, with threat to life a limb thrown in.

Some years ago, long after my time, the dreaded event took hold with disastrous results reducing Chapel and Dining Hall to mere shells but no one was hurt. That was because the school always had fire practices at least each term and sometimes twice. Once at night with smoke canisters for added realism, that was fun. But we never really knew if it were a practice or the real thing so responded wisely and quickly. The alarm bells would wake the dead. They were simple but effective, consisting of short lengths of steel girder suspended from hooks all over the school with metal hammers hanging close by. The racket the hammer made was deafening and the rule was "If you hear an alarm sounding and you are near another, sound it yourself until you hear others pick up the alarm and the school electric alarm bells begin to sound.

For some reason one morning I wanted to ask my housemaster a question, although I thought it most unlikely he would be "at home". I knocked on his study door and as custom was walked in. My surprise and horror at the smoke filled room made me step back abruptly. I could just see flames coming from the most comfortable settee in the room. Now I am inordinately proud of the next move. "Don't panic" shouts from the yet to be written Dad's Army came from me. Quickly shutting the door I ran to the nearby fire alarm and struck it wholeheartedly. What a delicious ear splitting racket! Then grabbing a passing youngster I gave him the task of going to the Porter's Lodge with the message of "Fire in Mr Field's study" And another boy took on the ringing of the alarm. Meanwhile all over the school alarms were ringing and the electric bells also informed me that the message had got through. Now, obedient boys, prefects and masters had to stop whatever they were doing, leave everything immediately and assemble in the Big Hall. Just for once I had ordered the life of the school including the Headmaster! Next with water bucket and of course courage, I entered the smoke filled room and began to douse the settee. It was quite a job until others came to help. Gracey was grateful and I felt quite a hero, which was not normal for me! Of course it was all quickly forgotten. A new settee replaced the burnt one but it wasn't quite so comfortable. Fire is really no fun whatever momentary excitement it causes.

BOMBS!

WHOOSH! How is it possible to describe the thump, thud, crack, crash, bang of an explosion which was then followed by the musical tinkling of broken glass on gravel? Impressive it certainly was. Everyone heard it. Yet there had been no warning. The sirens had not been sounded. Had the Germans perfected a completely silent and invisible plane to deliver a bomb? It was very odd.

Masters and Prefects dashed around like scaled cats looking for the scene of danger. This was in broad daylight. Ground floor covered, dormitories and Day Rooms investigated. Nothing amiss. Someone had the bright idea of going outside to look at the windows in search of the sound of broken glass. And there it was. In the New Science Wing. One window blown out. Yes, the explosion was home grown in the room where a machine turned petrol into gas suitable for our Bunsen burners. Science is like that. Kept under control it is very useful but given its head and out of control it goes wild. Rather like boys I suppose?

Delight Duty

Nothing escaped his eagle eye. He knew everyone and was in contact with the great world outside. He was neither a teacher, nor one of us, but someone standing, or rather sitting, as a link man between us all. He had no authority but that of supreme knowledge. Who was this great personage you ask? Who had this All Seeing Eye? Someone great? No, just a tough little gnome whose headquarters was just across the long corridor from the main door. The Porter. Through him letters came and went. He was the bringer of parcels and the carrier of serious messages such as "Report to the Headmasters study at once" He locked and unlocked doors, carried things, which is certainly the meaning of his title but as door-keeper he completed the full meaning of his trade.

There was, however, one part of his duty which a privileged few of us shared. There in the Porter's Lodge, with its wonderful coal fire, was the box of wires and switches and plugs which made up the internal telephone system. Hand operated of course. Here the chosen few sat on rota duty to take incoming calls and pass them on to whosoever was required. This duty was only in the evenings when the rest of the school were at evening meal and night time prep with heads down at books. It was good to be trusted. It was even better to be especially fed. One of the domestic staff would bring a tray brimming with hot food, also an individual tea pot, bread, butter and jam!

There were a few telephone calls, but not many, to disturb the solitary study time, or dream time, which naturally the warm coal fire induced so beautifully. Can you imagine the feeling of being somehow the hub of the College life for a few hours? Yours would be the responsibility of ringing for the police, ambulance, and fire brigade, if needed. Alone in your private world you were special and specially looked after doing your "homework" while everyone else was together being supervised in the Big School. Then having mastered the telephone system one could ring home, on reversed charges, and talk for a little to Dad! That was great. It was always with sorrow that we had to leave the Porter's Lodge and resume normal life, returning to the senior dorm when the night

Porter arrived, for there was a day porter as well to cover the 24 hours duty.

Drama

Acting on a stage. Now there's a memory. Lots of us acted. Some were acting all the time but this make-believe would be but a mask to cover up some turmoil or hurt, or just to bring laughter. But we really acted plays and very well at times. Indeed the Meynell House entertainment was, of course, better than that of the other Houses, although we never saw them nor they us. But that just must be so!

We did share in the greater plays put on before the whole school in the Big Hall and they were excellent to our eyes and always got a kindly write up in the College magazine. Even I was a bit overcome by the fulsome praise my attempt engendered after I had acted in "The Monkey's Paw". A delightful play with a bit of scary nail biting. I do recall the stunned silence my own horrified "faint" caused, it went on quite a time.

We also had visiting companies and one that I can still see was "Tobias and the Angel" This apocryphal story is, like most of the apocrypha, good drama, Daniel in "Bel and the Dragon" and The Story of Susanna" must be the original Sherlock Holmes. In "Tobias and the Angel" at one point we saw the Angel in his full colour, breathtaking in golden wings, massive in dignity, gigantic in voice, as still as a statue but pulsating with life, truly a messenger of God.

Sometimes visiting musical companies, mainly of the classical variety, introduced us to concerts and skills which we admired and began to appreciate. There is nothing like the real thing however good reproduction may be. That applies to the stage as to music although the cinema club did show some good films now and then.

The San'

Now and then illness struck. The German Measles outbreak went through the whole school. One of the dorms' was taken over as a hospital and we all trooped into it for a night or two as it progressed amongst us. It wasn't serious, disturbing yes, but as we were all in the same boat it had a bit of camaraderie about it. Colds and 'flu' could not be avoided but unless you really could prove a temperature there was no escaping school for the comfort of the Sanatorium and Matron's kindly strength. For she was both kind and strong and knew all about boys and what they were liable both to suffer and pretend to suffer.

I had scarlet fever inoculations while at school and was quite sick for two or three days as a result. Matron got to know my reaction so, as the course went on, called me into the San' for a bit of care and comfort until normality was established. With lesser troubles she had the usual spoonful of appropriate medicine for the usual upsets. I got quite a taste for quinine, due to being often snuffling with heavy colds. It's good stuff that and helped a bit. I can't say I've often heard of it being used these days, have you?

Darning

The sewing room was the only place that any of the boys ever met women not much older than themselves, or so we thought. These ladies spent their whole lives darning our socks. Socks were of wool in those days and usually went into holes at the heels within a few weeks of hard wear. But anything ripped, any lost buttons, they repaired and replaced. They also dished out our changes of clothing, sheets, towels and such like. As I said, certain older lads made special attempts to encourage dialogue with the younger element. I can't recall anything untoward happening as a result but then we would certainly not have been told about it if anything had occurred. We had to be protected from such things of course!

Intruder?

My Mum was shocked when she saw the college bathrooms. You will not be quite so taken aback, I expect. The thing that shocked her was that, in those days and until very recently, the bathroom was of the communal variety. A dozen or so deep baths down two sides of the one big bathroom. Everyone in clear view of the others. We sprang from the disrobing platform in the middle, where we hung up our pyjamas and dressing gowns, across the chilly concrete floor and into the steaming tubs as quickly as we could. As we only had a bath once a week we made the best of it. Delicious. And the water was Hot. Of course we had swilled ourselves under showers after games or, if we were seniors, plunged into a very large communal tub to chat over whatever sport had just exhausted us, so we did have other brushes with washing during the week. This was necessary as, you will remember, there was only cold water in the dormitory.

When it came to the time of my monthly shave I had to seek out the hot water tap at the wash basin just outside the bathroom. So this was in a wide corridor. This corridor led from our dormitory area past the bathroom and down a short flight of steps into the upper reaches of the newly opened Science wing.

Well there I was meditating on the amazing growth of fine hairs on my chin and scheming how to apply a good soapy froth with the shaving brush. I noticed a movement down in the darkened recesses of the corridor. Glancing round, there was the figure of a man! No one I knew. He saw me looking and vanished back into the Science wing so quickly I wondered if I had really seen him. With soapy face I went back into the dorm and reported the matter. What a hue and cry resulted! Prefects everywhere! The Science wing was searched, an open window discovered and a chase in the dark greatly enjoyed by the hunters. The fox, however, got away and must have informed other likely prowlers of the dangers, for we never had any further trouble of that sort.

I always keep my eyes open when shaving, you never know who or what is about the place.

Infuriating

My children used to find it hard to think of me running. Well, however hard it may seem to them, the truth is we all ran and sometimes ran very fast and I also ran, yes I did.

In the year previous to my being appointed in charge of House athletics we had some tough and unbeaten runners and as result most of the sports cups belonged to Meynell. John Brunt was one of them as I recall. Those of us remaining when he and the others left knew that our legs and stamina were not in the same class. The long distance race would be a severe test of our resources. The steeplechase, in particular, was a remarkable affair. The whole school took part. The scoring was by the simple expedient of counting the places of the first eight runners in each House and the House with the lowest score would be the winner. It was a team effort and no mistake. This meant that even those who came in 40th might, by overtaking the eighth boy from another House, put that team out of the running for the prize.

I knew this well. So with insistent words and

Churchillian tones about "*fighting to win in the lanes and along the tow path*" where the race led, and how "*England expects etc;-*" I enthused the House with speeches and we got ourselves organised into quite serious training.

On the day I had to run well, didn't I? Well I did my best but seven from other Houses came in long before I tottered to the finish, so it all depended on the energy of the rest of the House.

When the scores were totted up our total was one less than our nearest rival. Meynell had won! We had won by a whisker. The rest of the College was infuriated; they had very good runners. This infuriated them more. That was delightful to see although we very humbly told them it was a fluke. Ah, but was it? Churchillian spirit and Nelsonian grit helped towards our victory didn't it? Anyway the cup retained its Red Meynell marker for the next twelve months and that was what mattered.

Caught in the Act

It was good to be Captain of House. To go from the bottom of the lowest table in the House to the top of the highest table is a move greatly to be enjoyed. It brought responsibilities. But it also taught me a lesson which helped me when I entered the Fleet Air Arm as a 2nd Class Naval Rating right at the bottom of the Navy. Provided I worked at it there was the probability of progress. As indeed occurred in time.

Talking of responsibilities, they are heavy sometimes. By the way do you know about the details of cricket? For example there is the importance of being able to catch and hold the ball. I was never more than tolerably good at that, nor at throwing the little red leather globe far in the right direction. On second thoughts the direction got better but as for long distance I needed a backup fielder to get the ball from the boundary to the wicket. I enjoyed batting and bowling but was usually a short time at the crease where my stumps were particularly vulnerable. If I made contact with the ball and got two runs I claimed that to be a score in double figures.

Meynell was very short of senior cricketers that particular year. Thus it was, that very much against my will, I was brought into the team. After all as Captain of House I had a responsibility to perform bravely. When fielding, the team captain put me in a gentle enough position, middle and off I think. Not too far to throw if at any time I happened to stop a ball. We had made a reasonable score and I had got my double figures, something not to be sneezed at. We were on to the last pair and victory and the cup was in sight. It was then it happened, and to me it happened. Our fast bowler delivered a snorter. It clipped the hesitant edge of the lad batting number 11. Last man in. Scientifically it was obviously going to be a difficult catch but to the spectators it looked a gentle donkey drop into the safe hands of Captain of House, the Cup was ours! Don't you believe it. That ball leapt into the air in a curving, wobbling arch, hissing and whistling in acute agony, the speed of delivery was bad enough for its comfort but the sharp edge of the wood spun it into gyroscopic frenzy. It had a life all of its own. It had no desire or intention to spend any of it with me. It descended from on high towards me in an unsteady, jerky trajectory. My tentative hands reached out to grasp this red hot simmering devil. It thought nothing of my offer and decided immediately to depart. Depart it did, jumping aside as soon as it touched my palms with the agility of a startled cat, to cool its troubled nature on the cool green grass. I had dropped the catch that lost that match, which lost the cup. Ah well what burdens we leaders have to bear. Failure is one of them.

Problem Solving

He was a problem. He was not that small.
How did he get so dirty? It is expected that
boys become grubby. He remained grubby
even as he grew. Yes there was plenty of soap
about. Hand basins were available. His hands
just found other things to do and omitted
washing. Now that is quite all right if you live
by yourself like a hermit, but in a school,
when you can't get away from each other, it
becomes somewhat objectionable, especially
at table passing a bit of bread, for example.
Anyway there was a threat to the lad's own
health to consider.

"Wash your hands! Do it now! Show me your
hands!"
So it went on day after day, meal after meal.
No improvement.
"Write out hundreds of lines "I must wash my
hands before every meal""
He did that task but it made no impression on
the aforesaid talons. The House Prefects were
becoming frustrated. What to do?

As Captain of House "the problem" came to
me. He looked reasonable. I reasoned with

him. Nothing changed. He might very well just have been playing normally but as he never washed it looked as if his nails had been used to dig coal dust from the mud. I had to take "the problem" to the Housemaster.

"Well," he said. "Warn him again and tell him he will be beaten if he doesn't mend his ways i.e., wash his filthy hands."
I did.
He didn't.
I did again.
He still didn't.
"Do it," said my Housemaster. That is something I had no desire to do, but do it I had to! Richard Eccessley, then Captain of School, with whom I shared one of the two study rooms on the main corridor, stood by as witness to the beating. This was absolute law.

The "problem" came in.
"Bend over boy," said I, trying to be moderately tough.
He did.
"Whack," went my cane - the lad stood straight up, very pained.
"Bend over boy," said I. "And stay bent until I tell you to stand up."

He did.

"Whack" and "Whack," went the cane.

3 strokes. That was enough for me.

"Stand up. Always wash your hands before each meal. Go."

Go he did.

You will never have seen such spotless white hands!

His nails became immaculate.

We congratulated him.

The House Prefects were delighted. Problem solved.

A very few years later when I returned to pay a fleeting visit to the College, who should come down the main corridor towards me but the fine figure of a large and burly man. Now the "Problem" had himself become a Prefect of School in purple gown, happy and obviously in control of affairs. I had no need to look at his glistening finger nails I knew they would be white and pure as egg white, neatly beaten.

Lancing

Ellesmere College is one of a family of schools all founded by the endeavours of Canon Woodard. This, the senior College of the group, stands on a raised section of land near Lancing from which it draws its name. Of course Lancing is on the South coast of England looking towards the continent and therefore was in a danger zone from attack from the enemy. It was also an ideal spot to prepare for the invasion of the continent, whenever that should become possible. Therefore it could no longer function as a school and all the boys and teachers were evacuated.

So it was that, one summer term, the large lower playing field suddenly became a tented village for the senior element of Lancing College. Because they were so senior we had little or no dealings with them and, by a very clever juggling of time tables, both groups of boys hardly ever saw each other. The tented village was out of bounds to us and although its inhabitants used the science wing, and other facilities, the twain never did meet except on the cricket field. I expect the seniors of both schools had some contact but the term ended and come the autumn some other home had been found for Lancing. We got the larger playing field back for our own use. I should think that the boys of Lancing would have some fairly delicious stories to tell of their wartime adventures. I would like to read of them.

Swim?

Well yes if you like water but as I nearly drowned in the Gloucester swimming pool, when I had volunteered to be "saved" at some Scout competition, any desire I might have had to plunge into the water was severely limited. I found that if the water was really very hot, as in the tropics later on, I could make myself pretend I enjoyed a swim but I have to own that the cold, unheated pool at Ellesmere did not encourage me, although we all had to go in. At least the cold water forced me to be very active and therefore I did have a type of breast stroke which kept me warm, even if progress through the water had no relationship to the energy expended. Others, however, splashed about and swam lengths and played water polo for the inter-house games with evident enjoyment.

It was the pre breakfast swim that sorted out even the keenest of the keen ones. Off they ran across the top playing field to swim for twenty minutes or so, absolutely nude, to return glowing and terribly cheerful to scorn at us namby-pamby sleepy heads. I think you will understand that I did not mind being called anything rather than attempt to emulate their brave activity.

Squash-Gym

Now there is a game worthy of the name! I am so grateful that the College had a squash court and at a certain age I was encouraged to play. What energy! What skill! It was easy to find someone to play with and work out our frustrations on the little black ball, bashing it at clever angles against the walls. I think we had a competitive squash ladder to sort us out. There were also chess, billiard, table tennis, and tennis ladders. I was not good enough to get to the top of these, but that did not matter as those of us, having been defeated in the ladder, would continue to play amongst ourselves with great enjoyment. I was glad to have some skill in squash because both in the Navy in Ceylon and at University there were Squash courts. The game also helped me to play Rugby Fives and Eton Fives both of which do without the expense of rackets.

Gym times were greatly limited as I believe we were short of instructors at the time, although climbing ropes and wall bars were fun. The Gym was the place we sat in for our examinations, those awful times of trial on which so much depended for our futures. Having had a messed up start to my secondary education I have to praise the school for helping me do as well as I did scholastically, but I will not bore you with the results. Only to say that I was accepted for the Navy as a pilot, got into Durham University for a Science degree and followed that with two years at Cuddesdon Theological College before ordination in York Minster.

Haircut Sir?

There were a lot of things we could do for ourselves but no way could we manage to cut our own hair. Thoughtfully the college provided an itinerant Barber to cut his way through the school. He did this with gentleness and great speed and with such an eye for detail that although he carefully asked us "How would you like it done?" we all looked exactly the same when the job was completed. Well at least no one could be too proud or too ashamed of themselves afterwards and we all had a little bit of hair left to brush down or stick down, if we thought that was best. The queue of boys, controlled by a house prefect sat along the benches in the bathroom waiting for their individual execution. We had to pay 1/- (5p) for this privilege.

Toast

The Armoury had a stack of 303 rifles with which we had to drill when dressed in our Corps uniforms. They were of first War age but we had to clean them so often that they were in good condition. Of course there had to be an Armourer and that was my friend Slab. It was a real joy to visit him in his den and share a feast of toast and baked beans on the "brew up" ring he had there. There we talked much of the present war and what the current state of the battles implied. The rifle range next door was of special interest where we practised shooting 303 rifles, which had been adapted with 202 barrels, for indoor short range shots. It was by no means easy to hit the centre of the target, even at short range, but one or two boys were excellent shots. However, it was undoubtedly the hospitality of the armourer which I enjoyed the most, for every morsel taken between meals was indeed a bonus.

Half Days

We were at college for about twelve weeks at a time and for seven days every week, so any change in the steady routine was something much to be desired. The Half days on Wednesdays and Saturdays provided a break for us, and of course for the teachers, although we did not consider their needs at the time. These half days were spent playing games, writing letters, we had to write a letter home once a week by law, and if we had parents or family friends around we might even be taken out for an afternoon. Of course my parents were so far away that it was quite impossible for them to visit me at all, but I was given such a treat by a couple of visiting clergy. One was the General Secretary of the *Additional Curates Society* and the other belonged to the *Waifs and Strays*. He loved tea. In particular he liked to chew the tea leaves, which covered his red tongue with hundreds of black spots. He was one of the few clergy I know who enjoyed sticking his tongue out.

Sunday was very special. Disliked because we had to put on our dark suits and stiff collars. When young these were the massive Eton collars and when older we changed to the stiff, yes very hard, collars with rounded points, if you get my meaning. The Chapel services were of course compulsory and the singing often magnificent. Afterwards we had the day to ourselves including the compulsory walk in the winter terms and games in the summer. Those who had someone to take them off the premises spent the rest of the time enjoying some special delights and a sharing in home and school information. Why was it that I always seemed to start Mondays with Latin? That rather cast a shadow over the weekend.

Birds

You may recall the fact that the front quad walls were covered with very thick climbing Ivy. It reached up beyond our dormitory windows on the first floor and gave a delightful green look to what would otherwise be a mass of brickwork. The Ivy was a dormitory for birds. There must have been tens if not hundreds of nests and roosting places by the thousand. Maybe I exaggerate, but come the beginning of the summer term the dawn chorus was conducted by a very lively sun which had all the birds in full throat after one or two had acted as precentors. We needed no alarm bells or, maybe, we did, because 4 to 5 a.m. is a little early to expect lads to surface. I think we settled down for a second nap as the daylight increased.

Trunks

The trains ran from Oswestry to Whitchurch.
A line Dr. Beeching closed with many others
in the suicide of the railways. That line
brought nearly all of us to Ellesmere and then
began our journey home again. We had to
walk to the station of course, carrying as little
luggage as possible. All our clothes and
holiday work were sent on in trunks. Those
heavy trunks were man handled by the
railway staff and we paid 1/- or 5p for the
door to door delivery on top of the œ1 15/- I
think, for my return fare to Gloucester. That
is 175p which sounded a lot of money to me
then.

When we unpacked our trunks or needed to
pack them they were stored in the large void
above the corridor which led to our particular
bit of the school. It was quite a job stowing
them away and getting them out at end of
term. Senior boys with strong arms took the
job on when the men of the domestic staff
went away to the war. Well at least they were
empty trunks so it was a bit of fun rather than
a chore. In fact when they came down again
at the end of term we all brightened up

considerably looking forward to holidays and home cooking and adventures of all sorts. And, best of all, being HOME.

Onwards

Parting is a sorrow. Some leave school and are very glad that phase of life has ended. Others say it was the happiest years of their lives, having forgotten the nasty bits. I'm glad I remember bits good and not so good and some of them I have attempted to spell out in these Mere Memories.

My last term was rather special. The Head had honoured me by making me Prefect of Chapel and further clothing me in the purple gown, the highest "colour" of the school.

Like others of my age we were preparing to go immediately into the Armed Forces at the end of term, so we rather relished the freedom of the last days after exams, only being a bit sorry we could not go straight to University as would have been the case in peace time. But those days were to come after four years had passed. I suppose the visit my parents paid me that last term must have been as special for them as it was for me. Remember they had left me alone that January day years before, a lonely new boy and very ignorant of College life. Now I took them round the place as if it was all mine and shockingly proud of it I was too. For that matter I'm still proud of it. It might be worth your while calling in there one day, I'm sure there will be a Porter on duty, and if you ask nicely you might even get someone to take you round.

CPSIA information can be obtained
at www.ICGtesting.com
Printed in the USA
LVOW12s0031210118
563327LV00001B/78/P